Living Authentically

An Abundant Life Bible Study

by Cathy Schaefer & Tracy Wainwright

TLC Wainwright Publishing, LLC
VIRGINIA

Living Authentically

An Abundant Life Bible Study

Copyright © 2015 by Cathy Schaefer & Tracy Wainwright
Published by TLC Wainwright Publishing, LLC
P.O. Box 1001
Toano, VA 23168

All rights reserved. No part of this book may be reproduced, scanned, or distributed in any printed form or by any electronic or mechanical means, including information storage or retrieval systems, without permission in writing from the publisher, except by a reviewer who may quote brief passages in a review.

Unless otherwise indicated, all Scripture quotations are taken from the Holy Bible, New Living Translation, copyright © 1996, 2004, 2007 by Tyndale House Foundation. Used by permission of Tyndale House Publishers, Inc., Carol Stream, Illinois 60188. All rights reserved.

Cover Photo taken by Tracy Wainwright

Cover design by Rachel Piferi

ISBN-10: 0989948552
ISBN-13: 978-0-9899485-5-5

Contents

Week 1	*The Burden of Sin*	1
Week 2	*What are You Thirsting For?*	13
Week 3	*Confronted by Truth*	23
Week 4	*Amazing Grace*	31
Week 5	*Proclaim What the Lord has Done*	41
Closing Prayer		51
Endnotes		52

Week 1
The Burden of Sin

In a world where there are conflicting messages of "be who you are" and "put on your best face" (maybe you've seen all the articles, posts, and attention about retouching pictures in media), it is challenging to be authentic with everyone all the time.

Then we have our flesh that comes into play. And:

- Family values (like, "don't air your dirty laundry").
- What we perceive as everyone else having it all together.
- Wanting to keep our faults and failures out of the spotlight.

While on the surface, we try to be completely transparent, the truth is it's scary.

We, in our flesh, resist being completely open and honest for self-protection. We hide our flaws and failures from people around us.

Unfortunately, we also often try to hide them from God. Despite the fact that He calls us and invites us to lay all things bare before Him.

> Oh, what joy for those whose
> disobedience is forgiven, whose
> sin is put out of sight! Yes, what joy
> for those whose record the LORD
> has cleared of guilt, whose lives
> are lived in complete honesty!
> Psalm 32:1-2

> When I refused to confess my sin,
> my body wasted away, and I
> groaned all day long. Day and
> night your hand of discipline
> was heavy on me. My strength
> evaporated like water in the
> summer heat. Finally, I confessed
> all my sins to you and stopped
> trying to hide my guilt. I said to
> myself, "I will confess my rebellion
> to the LORD." And you forgave me!
> All my guilt is gone.
> Psalm 32:3-5

> O God, you know how foolish I am;
> my sins cannot be hidden from you.
> Psalm 69:5

Have you ever experienced the folly of trying to hide your guilt from God? I know I have! We know it's impossible to hide our sin from God, but we try to do it anyway. We run from Him, cover our guilt, deny that we have sinned, make excuses to justify our wrongdoing, ignore the pain, distract ourselves from the truth...anything to avoid facing our sin in front of a holy God.

Have you noticed the longer you avoid dealing with your guilt and shame, the harder it gets to face it?

We may learn to live with it, but it doesn't go away, it just gets stuffed down.

In an essay entitled "Spiritual warfare: Defeating guilt and shame" on the website GreatBibleStudy.com, I found this helpful description of the difference between guilt and shame:

"Guilt is what takes place when a person realizes their failure. . . . While guilt is seeing what you've done, shame is seeing yourself as a failure because of what you've done. Guilt is looking at the sin, shame is looking at yourself. If you allow yourself to meditate upon guilt, it will turn into shame. Guilt, if not properly dealt with, turns into a stronghold called shame."

Can you see the difference? This definition, along with scripture, shows us both the destruction sin brings in our lives and the beauty God's grace allows to blossom despite ourselves.

When we sin, mess up, fall short, get off the right path, our self-preservation desiring flesh tries to convince us to keep it hidden. We want to keep the masks up, pretending our dirt doesn't exist.

Has there been a time in your life you've hidden sin? If so, when was it and how did it affect you? (Either write on lines below, use a separate journal, or simply spend time reflecting.)

_____

_____

_____

_____

_____

The truth is, whenever we hide, cover up, or try to ignore sin, its negative impact compounds and multiplies. It continues to have a hold on us, often long after the natural consequences have passed.

If only we could grasp the freedom in repentance! To be real with each other so we know the truth that scripture tells us: No one is blameless and no one has it all together!

> For everyone has sinned; we all fall
> short of God's glorious standard.
> Romans 3:23

We often use this verse in witnessing, to show the lost that everyone is in the same boat. All of us have missed the mark of perfection that sets. However, it is also still true for those of us already saved by grace. We are saved, but we are also still human. In other words, even though we desperately desire to live a holy life, one pleasing to God and worthy of being called by His name, we still sin.

If you're human, you've suffered from feelings of guilt and shame at some time in your life. It is one of those unpleasant facts of living in a fallen world.

Guilt serves the purpose of convicting us of our sin in order that we will seek forgiveness and repent. **But** if we don't go directly to God with our guilt, it can turn to shame and affect the way we think about ourselves. And that's a problem, because instead of being more concerned with what God says about us, we can start to believe that we are defined by our sin, unworthy of God's love, and beyond hope, which is right where Satan wants us to stay.

When is a time you started believing Satan's lies about yourself?

_____

_____

_____

What did it take for you to see the truth – that nothing can separate you from God's love and mercy - through His grace? Or do you still need to?

_____

_____

_____

_____

When God created us, He made us to be thinking and feeling beings, with a whole spectrum of emotions. Guilt and shame didn't enter the picture, however, until after "The Fall." In fact, Genesis 2:25 tells us:

> Now the man and his wife were both
> naked, but they felt **no shame**.
> {emphasis added}

That is until after they sinned by eating the forbidden fruit.

Read Genesis 3:6-10

What was the first thing that happened after Adam and Eve sinned?

_____

_____

What did they do when they heard God approaching?

_____

_____

What emotion was Adam feeling in verse 10?

_____

Right after Adam and Eve sinned, *their eyes were opened*, and they clearly saw their deed for what it was – an act of disobedience against God. Prior to sinning, they had no knowledge of evil, but after sinning, they had knowledge of both good and evil.

Although the words guilt and shame aren't used in these verses, I think we can conclude that's what Adam and Eve experienced as a result of their sin.

Their guilt and shame caused them to:
1) Make *coverings for themselves* – suddenly they saw themselves differently, as naked and exposed, and vulnerable.

2) Hide from God – they didn't want God to know about their wrongdoing and tried to keep it from Him.

3) Feel afraid – they knew they had broken God's law and therefore deserved to be punished.

Before "The Fall," Adam and Eve had enjoyed a loving, intimate relationship with God. But their sin separated them from God and made them feel afraid.

I love the fact that, even though Adam and Eve had sinned against Him, God still came looking for them in the garden.

Did you catch that? God comes *looking for us* when we stray from Him!

He doesn't want us to run away and try to hide our sin from Him, cowering, alone and afraid. God wants to be in relationship with us, even when we feel guilty and ashamed. In fact, maybe even more so then!

He loves us too much to let us stay in the darkness, and

so He pursues us, in spite of our sin.

> My guilt overwhelms me – it is
> a burden too heavy to bear.
> Psalm 38:4

I have carried the burden of secret sin. "Burden" is a good description because the effort of hiding ~~your~~ sin weighs you down, saps your strength, and steals your peace and joy.

For 7 long years I carried the burden of my guilt and shame – buried it deep within myself and never spoke of it to anyone. But it was never far from my mind. I tried to run from it, but it always caught up with me, constantly reminding me that I was a failure and a fraud. If we don't take ~~your~~ sin directly to God, Satan will use it against us in an attempt to keep us in a prison of shame, far from the Lord.

Remember the question from a few pages ago, the one about a time you've hidden sin in your life. The effect on your spirit may have been the greatest of all, but also maybe the least acknowledged.

Did the cover-up take a toll on you? Did it cause you to feel afraid or distant from God? Explain.

_____

_____

_____

_____

Oftentimes we learn about God, His character, and how approachable He is from others who've been spiritual/church leaders in our lives. Sometimes people don't have a healthy, biblical view of God and don't present Him fully. This can affect how we feel when we sin, how we react, and our willingness to uncover it before God and seek His forgiveness.

Did you grow up with any misconceptions about God that made it more difficult to approach Him for grace and forgiveness? Explain.

_____
_____
_____
_____

Take a few minutes to read Psalm 139. Look closely at verses 1-4, 7 and 11-12.

Pick one or two of the verses that stand out most to you and write them below:

_____
_____
_____
_____
_____
_____
_____

What is the message to those hiding in the dark?

_____

_____

> Can anyone hide from me in a secret place? "Am I not everywhere in all the heavens and earth?" says the LORD.
> Jeremiah 23:24

Turn to Psalm 44:21. According to this verse, what does God know about us?

_____

_____

God knows us better than we know ourselves, and He is not surprised when we sin. He even knows what sins we are going to commit before we commit them.

Yet still He loves us, pursues us and desires to be in relationship with us.

Let that settle in, really settle to the depths of your soul. The God, Creator, and Sustainer of the universe pursues you despite knowing every sin you have and will ever commit.

Wow. That is truly worthy of the word amazing.

Take a few moments to reflect on God's infinite love, grace, and mercy. Praise Him for His character and how He heaps these things on us. Praise Him for every time He's forgiven you, sought you, or loved you.

Ask Him to reveal in you any hidden sin that needs to be uncovered, confessed. Lay everything before Him, not because He needs you to confess, but because it is healing to your mind, body, and spirit to do so. Lay it all down and thank Him for helping you take of the mask and be real with the Everlasting Father.

As you pray and reflect, use the space below as needed.

_____
_____
_____
_____
_____
_____
_____
_____

~~~*~~~

Those who look to Him are radiant;
their faces are never covered with shame.
Psalm 34:5

As Scripture says, "Anyone who believes
in Him will never be put to shame."
Romans 10:11

~~~*~~~

Week 1 Group Discussion Questions

(1) How does it make you feel to know that you were born with a sinful nature?

(2) What purpose does guilt serve in our lives

(3) When can guilt be helpful versus harmful?

(4) How does Satan use guilt against you?

(5) What are things we do or use to distract ourselves from facing our own sin?

(6) Why do you think it's so difficult to admit our sin to ourselves, God, or others?

(7) What are some ways God pursues us when we have strayed from Him?

Week 2
What Are You Thirsting For?

Have you ever been parched? Out in the hot sun for hours, nothing to drink, body starting to scream parched? I'm not sure many of us in America have had that extreme an experience. However, most of us have experienced thirst before.

Thirst is the body's craving for what is essential for life: water. Our physical bodies know how to signal us to seek what we need most. We get a dry mouth, headache, tight skin, and many other symptoms of dehydration. It tells us loud and clear what we're lacking!

Still, people end up in the hospital every day because they've ignored their body's signals and gotten to the point where they need help to replenish life-sustaining liquids to the body.

Our soul is similar, in that it gets parched without the Lord. When we have no connection, or have deprived that connection to the Living Water, our soul sends out signals of our needs.

Just as many ignore physical signs and symptoms of thirst, too many of us tend to disregard our spirit's warning signs that it is being neglected.

There is a reason for this: God created us to thirst for Him.

> As the deer longs for streams of water, **so I long for You, O God. I thirst for God, the living God.** When can I go and stand before him?
> Psalm 42:1-2
> {emphasis added}

> I lift my hands to you in prayer. **I thirst for You as parched land thirsts for rain.**
> Psalm 143:6
> {emphasis added}

> God blesses those who hunger and thirst for justice, for they will be satisfied.
> Matthew 5:6

When I was trying to do life "my way," apart from God, I was thirsty for truth and didn't even realize it. I was also thirsty for God's grace and forgiveness, but I didn't feel worthy to approach Him for it. First, I needed the truth about WHO He was and HOW MUCH He loved me. I needed to know that His amazing grace extended even to me, that His loving embrace was big enough to include me. I needed the reassurance that Jesus died for ALL our sins, even ones as awful as mine.

The awesome thing about Jesus is how very personal He is, how intimately He knows us. He will meet you where you are, in the midst of your ordinary, everyday life, and He will "speak" to you in a way that's specific to you with exactly what you need to hear most.

I love to read, and so one day in a bookstore, He led me to a book He knew I would be attracted to that could reveal His truth to me. The hope and encouragement I found in those pages was like a long drink of cool refreshing water to my world-weary thirsty soul.

Let's take a closer look at a story about another woman who was thirsty, and who was also well acquainted with guilt and shame.

Read John 4:3-9 and write a brief summary below. (It is a familiar story to many, so we want to be careful not to breeze by it and what God might want to teach us from it today.)

_____
_____
_____
_____
_____
_____

Samaria was situated between Judea and Galilee, and Jesus chose the shortest, most direct route, which would take them right through it.

According to Holman's Bible Dictionary, "In the days of

Christ, the relationship between the Jews and the Samaritans was greatly strained. The animosity was so great that the Jews bypassed Samaria as they traveled between Galilee and Judea. They went an extra distance through the barren land of Perea on the eastern side of the Jordan to avoid going through Samaria."

Yet Jesus chose differently.

While traveling through Samaria, Jesus and His disciples came to Jacob's well near a town called Sychar. The disciples went into the town for food, but Jesus sat down by the well to rest. As He waited, a Samaritan woman came to the well for water.

Don't miss the fact that this woman was just going about her normal, everyday routine, purposely visiting the well at a time of the day when it was usually deserted in order to be alone. But when she arrived at the well, Jesus was there waiting for her!

How has Jesus surprised you by showing up in the midst of your everyday life at a time when you needed Him?

_____
_____
_____
_____

Next, Jesus initiates a conversation with this Samaritan woman by asking her for a drink of water. Although fully divine, Jesus was also fully human, which meant that He was hot, tired and thirsty after His long journey on foot.

To the modern day reader, this request doesn't seem too unusual. But when seen against the backdrop of the religious, racial and cultural norms of the time, it is actually quite shocking that Jesus, a Jewish man, would strike up a conversation with a Samaritan woman (not to mention a woman with a bad reputation). But Jesus rarely does what is expected. His specialty is turning our worldly expectations upside down!

What do we know about this nameless woman? Not a lot, but we do know she had 3 strikes against her:

1) She was a Samaritan (considered inferior by the Jews)
2) She was a female in a public place alone (a cultural taboo)
3) She was a social outcast (a shameful woman with a bad reputation, despised and rejected by the other townspeople).

The other women in town came to the well to draw water when it was cooler, early in the morning or in the evening, and they chatted and visited as they carried out this daily chore. But this woman came to the well alone at the hottest part of the day, most likely in order to avoid the stares and whispers of the other women. I imagine she felt incredibly lonely, ashamed, and unworthy.

Holman's Bible Dictionary explains. "Honor and Shame were values that shaped everyday life in biblical times. . . . Women especially bore shame and were expected to do so in a positive manner. Women were also seen as threats to honor. An immoral woman tainted the honor of the entire family, and so women generally were kept away from things tending to dishonorable behavior. The veiling of women related to this concern."

What do you think this woman's greatest need might have been when she encountered Jesus?

_____

_____

Aside from her obvious physical need for water, I can think of a few other needs she may have had:

    1) Acceptance – since others judged and rejected her.
    2) True Love – since she had already "loved and lost" 5 husbands.
    3) Forgiveness – since she bore the shame of "living in sin" with another man she wasn't married to.
    4) Kindness – since others despised and avoided her.
    5) Friendship – since she lived the solitary life of a social outcast.

I don't know about you, but although I dearly love my

husband and children, I simply cannot imagine my life without my girlfriends. They love and accept me in spite of my faults, and the support and encouragement they offer me are invaluable. It does my soul good to spend time talking over problems big and small with them. (And spares my husband the effort of trying to listen to all my "verbal processing!")

Try to imagine the lonely existence of this Samaritan woman. She has been through a series of relationships with several men, who may or may not have loved and/or mistreated her, and now she must come to the well alone to escape the rejection and judgment of the other women in town. How she must have longed for one true friend!

Have you ever known the pain and isolation of feeling judged, rejected, ashamed or unworthy? How did you deal with that?

_____
_____
_____
_____
_____
_____

What are you currently "thirsting for?" What is your greatest need right now?

_____
_____

In order to live a truly authentic life, we need to not only bring our sin and repentance to the Lord, but also our needs. He desires that we be honest and open about our longings, and that we long for Him most of all. That we stop trying to cover our empty spiritual places with things physical and/or emotional.

Too often we try to assuage our thirst with:
- Relationships
- Food
- Distraction
- Accomplishments
- Busyness
- Drugs and alcohol
- Material possessions
- Careers
- (you fill in the blank) _____

Instead of turning to anyone or anything else for sustenance, Jesus is calling us to Himself to quench our thirst.

Use the lines below to ask God to make your greatest craving be for Him.

_____
_____
_____
_____
_____

~~~*~~~

From the depths of despair, O Lord;
I call for your help. Hear my cry, O
Lord. Pay attention to my prayer. Lord,
if You kept a record of our sins, who O
Lord, could ever survive? But you offer
forgiveness, that we might learn to
fear you. O Israel, hope in the Lord;
for with the Lord there is unfailing
love His redemption overflows.
Psalm 130:1-4, 7

Turn to me and have mercy, for
I am alone and in deep distress.
Psalm 25:16

~~~*~~~

Week 2 Group Discussion Questions

(1) What is the deep thirst of every human soul?

(2) Why is it so difficult for us to correctly identify our spiritual thirst?

(3) What are some of the misguided ways we attempt to satisfy the thirst of our soul?

(4) How can fear prevent us from an authentic, intimate relationship with Jesus Christ?

(5) What does it mean to "fear the Lord?" How does it differ from our usual concept of fear?

(6) Why are we so often reluctant to take our deepest needs and desires to the Lord?

Week 3
Confronted by Truth

Have mercy on me, O God, because of your unfailing love. Because of your great compassion, blot out the stain of my sins. Wash me clean from my guilt. **For I recognize my rebellion; it haunts me day and night. Against you, and you alone, have I sinned; I have done what is evil in Your sight. You will be proved right in what you say and your judgment against me is just. For I was born a sinner – yes, from the moment my mother conceived me. But you desire honesty from the womb, teaching me wisdom even there.** Forgive me for shedding blood, O God who saves; then I will joyfully sing of your forgiveness. Unseal my lips, O Lord, that my mouth may praise you. You do not desire a sacrifice, or I would offer one; You do not want a burnt offerings. **The sacrifice you desire is a broken spirit. You will not reject a broken and repentant heart, O God,.**
Psalm 51:1-6,14-17
{emphasis added}

> Those who love their life in this world will lose it.
> Those who care nothing for their life in this
> world will keep it for eternity.
> John 12:25

When I was weighed down by the guilt and shame of my sin, I longed to be free of my burden. But I was convinced that my sin was too serious, that I was beyond hope. I had assigned myself as judge and jury over my own case, and I had rendered the verdict of "guilty as charged." Case closed.

My assessment of my sinful state as hopelessly doomed was correct – in part.

Little did I know, I was right where I needed to be: I HAD COME TO THE END OF MYSELF.

The time had come to "get real with myself" and face the truth: the burden of my guilt and shame were too much to bear, and I was BROKEN. I was a Sinner in need of a Savior.

Let's return to the woman at the well, who I suspect may have also been a woman who was broken and at the end of herself. Read John 4:9-19

The Samaritan woman is shocked that Jesus would ask her for a drink, and she says so. For a Jew to accept food or drink from a Samaritan made them ceremonially unclean. Jesus calls Himself *the gift of God*, and describes *living water*.

Read Romans 6:23, and write the verse here:

_____

_____

_____

_____

What is *the gift of God?*

_____

_____

Jesus even claims that, "whoever drinks the water I give him will never thirst."

The woman is intrigued. She would like some of this water so she doesn't have to keep making daily trips to the well! She is focused on her physical need for water and doesn't realize Jesus is more interested in satisfying her spiritual thirst.

Have you ever wished that Jesus would make your life easier by providing more for your physical needs?

_____

_____

What do you pray for more often – your physical needs or your spiritual needs? Why?

_____

_____

_____

The conversation takes an interesting turn in John 4:16 when Jesus asks her to go get her husband. I have to give her credit for being "real." She is truthful and doesn't try to deny or make excuses for her sins. I think that in her shame-filled condition, this is as close as she can get to a confession. She admits she has no husband without going into detail about her past marriages, or her current relationship.

Can you imagine conversing face-to-face with Jesus?

With *the Word made flesh* standing before you, I doubt it would be possible to be anything less than completely honest. Do you think she had the courage to look into His eyes? The Bible tells us that there was nothing exceptional about His physical appearance, but I have to believe that His eyes must have been intense, piercing, mesmerizing even. It's been said the eyes are a reflection of one's soul. If that's true, Jesus must have had the most amazingly beautiful eyes ever!

The woman must have felt as if Jesus was looking directly into her soul when He revealed that He knew all about her past. Yet what He *doesn't* say is almost as important as what He *does* say. He doesn't judge her, berate her, belittle her, or condemn her. He acknowledges her sin, but doesn't leave or reject her because of it. How surprising (and even freeing) it must have been for her to realize that He accepted her as she was, in all her sin, and was willing to remain engaged in conversation with her in spite of it.

If you were at the well, what would Jesus know about you? (If you're not ready to write it here, spend some time in contemplative thought and prayer.)

_____
_____

Is there an area of your life where you have come to the end of yourself? Are you ready to turn your burden over to God? What is preventing you from doing so? Use the space below to answer the questions and/or offer a prayer up to the Lord asking to help remove any barriers from laying down your burden.

_____
_____
_____
_____
_____
_____
_____

Read Luke 5:31-32

Who does Jesus say He came to call?

_____

We all qualify. Every one of us. Won't you open yourself to His complete healing? The healing He desires to give us goes beyond salvation, but also allows reveals, rescues, and restores us from everything!

~~~*~~~

The L ORD is close to all who call on him,
yes, to all who call on Him in truth. He grants
the desires of those who fear him; he hears
their cries for help and rescues them.
Psalm 145:18-19

Then Jesus said, "Come to me, all of you
who are weary and carry heavy burdens,
and I will give you rest. Take my yoke
upon you. Let me teach you, because
I am humble and gentle at heart, and
you will find rest for your souls. For my
yoke is easy to bear, and the
burden I give you is light."
Matthew 11:28-30

The Spirit and the bride say, "Come."
Let anyone who hears this say, "Come."
Let anyone who is thirsty come.
Let anyone who desires drink freely
from the water of life.
Revelation 22:17

~~~*~~~

Week 3 Group Discussion Questions

(1) Do you think we tend to judge ourselves more or less harshly than God judges us? Why?

(2) Have you ever felt that you needed to "clean yourself up" before you could approach God? Why is this thinking so dangerous?

(3) What do you most fear or joyfully anticipate about the day when you will meet Jesus face to face? Why?

(4) What is the most important or meaningful aspect of God's character to you? Why?

(5) Why is it crucial that we "come to the end of ourselves" and admit our brokenness?

Week 4
Amazing Grace

Let all that I am praise the Lord; May I never forget the good things he has done for me. He forgives all my sins and heals all my diseases. He redeems me from death and crowns me with love and tender mercies. He fills my life with good things. My youth is renewed like the eagle's! The Lord gives righteousness and justice to all who are treated unfairly. The Lord is compassionate and merciful, Slow to get angry and filled with unfailing love. He does not punish us for all our sins; he does not deal harshly with us, as we deserve. For his unfailing love toward those who fear him is great as the height of the heavens above the earth. He has removed our sins as far from us as the east is from the west. The Lord is like a father to his children, tender and compassionate to those who fear him.
Psalm 103:2-6,8,10-13

If we claim to have no sin, we are only fooling ourselves and not living in the truth. **But if we confess our sins to him, he is faithful and just to forgive us our sins and to cleanse us from all wickedness.**
1 John 1:8-9
{emphasis added}

Take a moment to reread these verses. Underline specific words or phrases that stand out to you as you soak them in. You can also use the lines below to write down anything that God is reminding you or revealing to you for the first time.

_____
_____
_____
_____
_____

I think we all too often rush through the awesomeness of God's grace and mercy. Let us not do that today. Instead let us feast on them, filling our spirits to their very cores.

Once you've gone through the above verses meditatively and intentionally, I recommend that you also pray through them. Use them as a basis to start today's session. Write your prayer below if you feel led:

_____
_____
_____
_____

Once I was convicted of my sin and brokenness and recognized my need for Jesus, I knew that the next step was to "get real" with God – go before Him in humble submission, confess my sins, and ask His forgiveness. But I didn't do it right away because frankly, I was afraid. The idea of going directly to God was a bit intimidating.

I was afraid of His power and authority, afraid that He

might ignore, punish or reject me, afraid of what would be required of me if He did forgive me. . . . Looking back, it seems kind of silly, but that's how confused my thinking was at the time.

How grateful I am that God continued to remind me of my need until I finally bowed before Jesus, tearfully poured out my humble and sincere confession, and begged Him to be Lord of my life. I was rewarded with a response of the most incredible love, mercy, compassion and grace!

As soon as the words were out of mouth, my burden of guilt and shame was lifted and replaced with a deep sense of peace, indescribable joy, and Amazing Grace!

The Holman Bible Dictionary's definition of repentance is, "Change of mind; . . . a shift or reversal of thought. In its biblical sense repentance refers to *a deeply seated and thorough turning from self to God*. It occurs when a radical turning to God takes place, an experience in which God is recognized as the most important fact of one's existence."

How beautiful a picture that is of repentance! It's not just so we can be forgiven and renewed, but an experience where the Lord, Creator, Savior, Holy God, Almighty, Heavenly Father becomes more real than anything else in life.

Read James 4:6. Who does God give grace to?

Have you acknowledged your deep need for Jesus and repented (turned from self to God)? What were the circumstances that led you to that place?

_____
_____
_____
_____

What are some of the benefits of being reconciled to God?

_____
_____
_____
_____
_____

Let's resume our story of the Woman at the Well by reading John 4:17-26

I find it interesting that the Samaritan woman doesn't leave or end the conversation after Jesus exposes her sin. I think she must have been drawn to His compassion and gentleness.
Throughout their entire encounter, Jesus treats her with such kindness and respect, such love and grace. She is obviously impressed by Him, and declares Him to be a prophet. She must have been thoroughly convinced

that He possesses some spiritual authority.

But she also seems eager to change the subject, and asks Him a question about the correct place to worship. Jesus doesn't answer the question directly, but explains that the more important issue is the correct heart attitude for worship because "God is spirit, and His worshipers must worship in spirit and in truth."

It's unclear if the woman fully grasped the meaning of His words, but she seemed to know something of the Scriptures and asserted her belief that "Messiah is coming. . .he will explain everything to us."

Read Romans 10:10 and write it here:

_____

_____

_____

_____

I suggest to you that in verse 25 of our main passage, the woman at the well is professing her faith, and Jesus rewards her faith by revealing His true identity! If there was ever a "least likely" candidate Jesus could choose to make such a profound announcement to, she would be it: a female, a despised Samaritan (enemy of the Jews), a social outcast and a known sinner.

But Jesus is only concerned with one thing – the condition of the heart.

> People may be right in their own eyes,
> But the Lord examines their heart.
> Proverbs 21:2

What is the current condition of your heart? How would you describe the depth and breadth of your belief in and devotion to God?

_____

_____

_____

_____

Have you professed Jesus as Lord and turned your life over to Him?

What are some of the ways that He has revealed Himself to you?

_____

_____

_____

_____

How has your life changed since you turned it over to Jesus?

_____

_____

_____

_____

How have/do you show Him your love and gratitude?

_____

_____

_____

_____

There is no greater joy for a human being than to have an authentic relationship with Jesus Christ – to have a heart that is fully surrendered and completely committed to Him!

He came to *set the captives free*, and He doesn't want to see you enslaved to sin. He sees you in your sin and brokenness and loves you still. He had such love for you that He went to the cross for you *while you were still a sinner (Romans 5:8).*

We can't clean ourselves up – either for salvation or for sanctification - only the blood of Jesus can wash us clean.

Jesus loved you so much that He came to earth to do for you what you could not do for yourself.

Write Ephesians 2:13 here:

_____

_____

_____

_____

_____

How great is His love for us!

Pick one verse from this week to write on a card and keep close by. Review it often and use the Living Word to remind you of His amazing, perfect love each and every day.

~~~*~~~

So now no condemnation for those who belong Christ Jesus. And because you belong to him, the power of the life-giving Spirit has freed you from the power of sin that leads to death.
Romans 8:1-2

For this is how God loved the world: He gave his one and only Son, so that everyone who believes in him will not perish but have eternal life. God sent his Son into the world not to judge the world, but to save the world through him.
John 3:16-17

~~~*~~~

Week 4 Group Discussion Questions

(1) How would you define or describe God's grace to an unbeliever?

(2) Why is God's grace more important than God's law? How do they work together to bring about our repentance and salvation?

(3) Why don't more people accept the free gift of grace and forgiveness offered by Christ?

(4) Which do you think is more difficult: accepting God's forgiveness for our sins, or forgiving ourselves for sinning?

(5) Why do we so often continue to "stand accused" and live in shame, even after confessing and receiving assurance of God's grace and forgiveness? Why is that an insult to the work Christ did on the cross?

(6) What is the most effective way to deal with ongoing attacks from Satan, "the accuser?"

Week 5
Proclaim What the Lord Has Done

There is danger in a long-term relationship with Jesus. He never changes and is always faithful, but we tend to get distracted from Him. Even after we've embraced His love, mercy, and grace, we slip back into behaviors, thoughts, and words that aren't glorying to Him. They contradict His perfect behavior and threaten to put us in, or keep us in, a dark pit.

Yet we know we are saved and we call ourselves by His name. This may tempt us even greater to put on masks and try to hide our flaws and failures. To live behind a false presentation of who we really are.

Sin always festers in the dark. It's not only important for us to confess to the Lord, but He also directs us to confess to each other.

> Confess your sins to each
> other and pray for each other
> so that you may be healed.
> James 5:16a

In doing this, we shed the light on our sin. Not just the light of the truth, but the light of the Son. We have the opportunity to face our worst fears and survive. We have a greater opportunity to be surrounded by the love and support of our brothers and sisters. We do make ourselves vulnerable to judgement and scorn, but those reactions would only come from those who haven't truly grasped God's grace.

But in the pulling back the curtain on the mud and muck of our lives we also have a much greater opportunity: *to be a living example of God's mercy and grace and bring more glory to His name!*

> Give thanks to the Lord, for He is good;
> His faithful love endures forever.
> **In my distress I prayed to the Lord, and**
> **the Lord answered and sett me free.**
> The Lord is for me, so I will have no fear.
> What can mere people do to me?
> Yes, the Lord is for me; he will help me.
> My enemies did their best to kill me,
> But the Lord rescued me. The Lord
> is my strength and my song;
> he has given me victory.
> **I will not die; instead, I will live**
> **to tell what the Lord has done.**
> The Lord is God, shining upon us.
> Give thanks to the Lord, for He is good!
> His faithful love endures forever.
> Psalm 118:1,5-7,13-14,17,27a,29
> {emphasis added}

> **Your unfailing love is better than life itself;**
> **How I praise you!** I will praise you as long as
> I live, lifting up my hands to you in prayer.
> You satisfy me more than the richest feast.
> I will praise you with songs of joy.
> Psalm 63:3-5
> {emphasis added}

> And you will know the truth,
> and the truth will set you free.
> John 8:32

If Jesus has "set you free" from the bondage of sin, then you have a story to tell, and one of the best ways to show your gratitude is to proclaim what the Lord has done.

Why are we so eager to share our good news about an engagement, a new baby, a job promotion, or our child's success on the athletic field, but when it comes to victories in our spiritual life, we so often stay quiet and keep it to ourselves?

I am not pointing fingers here because I am guilty of this too. But in my heart of hearts I fear that maybe God's biggest disappointments with me might not be about the things *I did say that I shouldn't have*, but instead the things *I didn't say that I should have*.

Specifically those times when I didn't speak up to defend His name, or failed to share the hope and truth of Jesus with a lost and hurting soul.

He has done marvelous things for me! I was broken, but Jesus has healed me and made me whole! I was imprisoned by my sin, but He has set me free! I once was blind, but now I see! I was condemned to die, but have received forgiveness and the free gift of eternal salvation!

Jesus is my best friend and also Lord of my life. He helps me every single day in ways big and small. He gives my life meaning and purpose, and I can't imagine my life without Him.

HOW can I keep such good news to myself when the world is filled with so many lost, sick, sad and broken people? This is a question I want to keep in the forefront of my life every day, and as we finish our story of the Woman at the Well.

Read John 4:25-43.

Immediately after Jesus reveals to the Samaritan woman that He IS the Messiah, his disciples return with lunch! There is no record of her response. Perhaps that's because she likely had *no words* at that moment: Standing in the presence of the Messiah. Can you even imagine?!

Then, forgetting her water jar (because her need for physical water pales in comparison to having her spiritual thirst quenched by the *Living Water*), she heads back to town to share this exciting news with others.

Although she doesn't respond to Jesus verbally, her actions indicate that she BELIEVES.

Healing comes through believing.

Let's look at another woman who had a bit more brief interaction with the Savior of this world. We find this encounter in Luke 8:48. What did Jesus say to the bleeding woman?

_____

The woman of blood was healed and changed by her encounter with Christ.

So was the woman at the well. She also gained the courage to *act* on her faith. What a turn-around! She forgets herself, her past, her reputation, because it no longer defines her. Other people's opinions become less important than the urgency and importance of her message! Her message was, and still is compelling, and people listened.

I have to think the change in her demeanor and personality must have been compelling as well. Is it possible her testimony had more impact because of her bad reputation? Who could resist the opportunity to meet the man who knew all about this woman's sinful past?

What stands out to you in verses 39-42?

_____

_____

By the end of the story, she is back in community. Other townspeople are talking to her; she is in relationship with them. Jesus validates her, restores her dignity, and she even seems to have gained some new-found respect with the people of her town. Because she met the Great Physician and received healing, she was able to share the source of her hope and encourage others to find hope and healing in Him as well.

No doubt about it, it's scary to risk "getting real with others" by sharing our story and revealing our pain and brokenness. I've been there. I get it. But I can also assure you that every time I have stepped out in faith and shared my pain and brokenness with others, I have been richly rewarded.

Being authentic with others allows them to do the same with you, and then you have the greatest opportunity to introduce them to Jesus, the Great Healer.

I recently came across this quote on Facebook (no source listed): *God often uses our deepest pain as the launching pad of our greatest calling.*

What is the source of your deepest pain?
_____

Do you think God might be asking you to share your pain in order to minister to others? _____

According to 2 Corinthians 1:3-4, what is one of the

reasons that *God comforts us in all our troubles?*

_____

_____

Are you willing to set aside concerns about your own reputation in order to offer comfort to others? What might this look like?

_____

_____

_____

"When we deny the story, it defines us. When we own the story, we can write a brave new ending."
~Brene' Brown

My friend, the pain and brokenness in your life don't define you! If you are *in Christ,* you are a new creation (2 Cor. 5:17) and Jesus has provided a brave new ending to your story! Own it, for through Him, we are more than conquerors! (Romans 8:37)

> We know what love is because Christ
> gave his life for us. We should give our
> live for our brothers (*and sisters*).
> 1 John 3:16
> {words in parenthesis added}

~~~*~~~
Instead, you must worship Christ as Lord
of all your life. And if someone asks
about your hope as a believer,
always be ready to explain it.
1 Peter 3:15
~~~*~~~

Week 5 Group Discussion Questions

(1) What are some ways that we receive comfort from Christ?

(2) Why are we often so reluctant to share the "good news" of the gospel with others?

(3) What are some factors or circumstances that make it easier for us to share Christ with others? Can you think of a time or a situation when you successfully did so?

(4) Why is it most effective to share your story/personal testimony?

(5) Is it easier for you to show the love of Christ to others through your words or through your actions? Is one more important than the other? Why or why not?

(6) Why is an authentic relationship with Christ critical to witnessing effectively?

Closing Prayer

Lord Jesus, I pray that we would humbly and honestly confess our painful pasts, our secret sins, and our daily struggles to You in order to receive the forgiveness and healing that only You can give. May we be so utterly and completely transformed by our encounters with You, Christ, that we become more concerned about sharing the Good News of the gospel than in protecting our own reputations. Fill us with Your Holy Spirit, Lord, so that Your love and light will be evident to all. Help us to always be willing to share the reason for the hope that is in us with the thirsty people we meet each and every day. By Your Power and Might, Lord. Amen.

With deep gratitude to Jesus Christ, my Lord and Savior.
~Cathy Schaefer

Endnotes

Week 1

1. "Spiritual warfare: Defeating guilt and shame," from the website Great Bible Study.com, www.greatbiblestudy.com/SWS_guilt_shame.php, copyrighted 2003-2008 by Robert L. Boldt and its licensors

Week 2

2. "Samaria, Samaritans," by Donald R. Potts, Holman Illustrated Bible Dictionary, copyright 2003 by Holman Bible Publishers, Nashville, TN; General Editors: Chad Brand, Charles Draper, Archie England

3. "Shame and Honor," by Bill Warren, Holman Illustrated Bible Dictionary, copyright 2003 by Holman Bible Publishers, Nashville, TN; General Editors: Chad Brand, Charles Draper, Archie England

Week 4

4. "Repentance," by Clark Palmer, Holman Illustrated Bible Dictionary, copyright 2003 by Holman Bible Publishers, Nashville, TN; General Editors: Chad Brand, Charles Draper, Archie England

Week 5

5. RISING STRONG: The Reckoning, The Rumble, The Revolution by Brene' Brown, copyright 2015, Published by Spiegel & Grau, a division of Penguin Random House LLC, New York

www.ingramcontent.com/pod-product-compliance
Lightning Source LLC
Chambersburg PA
CBHW061257040426
42444CB00010B/2410